D1251975

Finding My Elegy

Selected Books by Ursula K. Le Guin

FICTION

A Wizard of Earthsea

The Left Hand of Darkness

The Tombs of Atuan

The Lathe of Heaven

The Farthest Shore

The Dispossessed

The Word for World Is Forest

Very Far Away from Anywhere Else

Malafrena

The Beginning Place

The Eye of the Heron

Always Coming Home

Searoad

Tehanu

The Telling

Four Ways to Forgiveness

Unlocking the Air

Tales from Earthsea

The Other Wind

Gifts

Voices

Powers

Lavinia

POETRY

Wild Angels

Walking in Cornwall
  (chapbook)

Tillai and Tylissos
  (with Theodora Kroeber; chapbook)

Hard Words

In the Red Zone
  (with Henk Pander; chapbook)

Wild Oats and Fireweed

No Boats (chapbook)

Blue Moon over Thurman Street

Going Out with Peacocks

Sixty Odd

Incredible Good Fortune

TRANSLATION

Lao Tzu: Tao Te Ching

Selected Poems of Gabriela Mistral

Finding My Elegy

New and Selected Poems
1960–2010

Ursula K. Le Guin

Houghton Mifflin Harcourt
Boston   New York
2012

For information about permission to reproduce selections from this book,
write to Permissions, Houghton Mifflin Harcourt Publishing Company,
215 Park Avenue South, New York, New York 10003.

www.hmhbooks.com

Library of Congress Cataloging-in-Publication Data
Le Guin, Ursula K., date.
  Finding my elegy : new and selected poems 1960–2010 / Ursula K. Le Guin.
    p. cm.
  ISBN 978-0-547-85820-3
  I. Title.
  PS3562.E42F55 2012
  811'.54—dc23   2012016363

Book design by Lisa Diercks

Printed in the United States of America
DOC 10 9 8 7 6 5 4 3 2 1

All of the poems in Part I and some poems in Part II previously appeared in the following
books: *Wild Angels* (Capra, 1974). *Tillai and Tylissos* (chapbook, with Theodora Kroeber; Red
Bull, 1979). *Hard Words* (Harper & Row, 1981). *In the Red Zone* (chapbook, with Henk Pander;
Lord John, 1983). *Buffalo Gals and Other Animal Presences* (Capra, 1987). *Wild Oats and Fireweed*
(Harper & Row, 1988). *No Boats* (chapbook; Ygor & Buntho Make Books Press, 1991). *Blue
Moon over Thurman Street* (with Roger Dorband; NewSage, 1993). *Going Out with Peacocks*
(HarperCollins, 1994). *Sixty Odd* (Shambhala, 1999). *Incredible Good Fortune* (Shambhala, 2007).
Four Different Poems (chapbook; Longhouse, 2007). *The Wild Girls* (PM Press, 2011).

The following poems first appeared in these publications: *Amicus Journal* (1991): "Riding the
'Coast Starlight.'" *Attic* (2003): "The Lost Explorer," "A Measure of Desolation." *Breaking
Waves*/Book View Café (2003): "In England in the Fifties." *Calapooya Collage* (1991): "The
Pacific Slope." *Cream City Review* (1993): "The Queen of Spain . . ." *Grove Review* (2003):
"Here, There, at the Marsh." *International Dream Quarterly* (1993): "Waking: Two Poems."
Lady Churchill's Rosebud Wristlet (2003): "Watching the Fractal Set." *Milkweed Chronicle*
(1987): "Inventory." *Moral Ground*/Trinity University Press (2011): "The Conference" (as
"The Conference of Time"). *Northwest Review* (2007): "Finding My Elegy." *Off the Coastal
Path*/Stanza Press (2010): "Creation of the Horse." *Open Places* (#33, 1982): "Wild Oats and
Fireweed." Oregon Environmental Council newsletter: "Coast Range Highway." *Oregon
Literary Review* (2006): "At the Clackamas County Fair" (as "Sapphics at the Clackamas County
Fair"), "Diamond Gravel" (as "Diamond Gravel Dialogue"). *Papers, Inc.* (1974): "Tao Song"
(as "Tao Poem"). *Peace and Freedom* (2009): "Curse of the Prophetess." *Ploughshares* (2010):
"Hour of the Changes," "Votum." PoetryMagazine.com (2003): "Talk Shows." *Poets Against
the War* (2003): "American Wars." *Portland Review* (2010): "The Greater Forest." *Realms of
Fantasy* (2011): "Distance," "Mendenhall Glacier." *Stone Telling* (2011): "The Elders at the Falls."
Villanelle/Modern Library (2012): "Extinction." *Windfall:* "At Kishamish" (11 poems; 2011),
"Red Alders in March" (2008). Women's International League for Peace and Freedom (1987):
"The Vigil for Ben Linder."

Contents

LIFE SCIENCES: NEW POEMS, 2006–2010

I. *Socioesthetics*

I

Wild Fortune

Selected Poems, 1960–2005

From Wild Angels *(1960–1975)*

Offering

I made a poem going
to sleep last night, woke
in sunlight, it was clean forgotten.

If it was any good, gods
of the great darkness
where sleep goes and farther
death goes, you not named,
then as true offering
accept it.

A Lament for Rheged

Frozen thorn,
grey north, white hill.
Winter binds
reeds, rivers. Everything
holds still.

Who has returned
in the bitter weather
to the place of birth?
The fire burned
here. Under the frozen earth
and the white frost,
this was the hearth.

Of all the lost
children I was chosen
to return. No choice
of mine! I chose to sing.
The lark's part,
the bard's. The wing,
the voice, must sink, be still.
Lark to the earth,
I to the hearth
under the cold hill.

I was not born noble
but a bondsman

bound to the land.
Hold still. Hold still.

Winter wind
binds eye, binds hand.

Who will remember?
A place of birth,
a place of marriages,
the household of summer.
Who will praise
the work, the kindness,
the full table,
the hearth of stone?

In the cold days
of the end of December
in dead Rheged
I stand alone.

Winter wind
binds hand, binds tongue.
The songs are sung.
No fires burn.

Yet I return
to the winter land

having chosen
the heavy art,
the bond of thing,
of stone, of earth.
I am bound to stand
under the frozen
thorn, by the cold
hearth, and sing.

There

He planted the elms, the eucalyptus,
the little cypress, and watered them
in the long dusk of summer,
so that in the dry land
twilight was a sound of water. Years ago.
The amaryllis stick their stiff
trumpets still blowing blasts of bright pink
up through the wild oats,
unwatered, uncounted, undaunted.

    Do you see: there where his absence
stands by each tree waiting for nightfall,
where shadows are his being gone, there
where grey pines that no one planted
grow tall and die, and grain that no one sowed
whitens the August hills with wild ripeness,
and an old house stands empty,
there
the averted face of absence
turns. There silence returns answer. There
the years can go uncounted, seeing
evening rise like water through the leaves,
and as ever over the highest elm Vega
like a wild white poppy, opening.

    In the country of pain
truly there only rises
(a white star, a white flower,
an old standpipe running water
to the roots of trees
in a dry land)
the small spring of peace.

Ars Lunga

I sit here perpetually inventing new people
as if the population boom were not enough
and not enough terror and problems
God knows, but I know too,
that's the point. Never fear enough
to match delight, nor a deep enough abyss,
nor time enough, and there are always a few
stars missing.

I don't want a new heaven and new earth,
only the old ones.
Old sky, old dirt, new grass.
Nor life beyond the grave,
God help me, or I'll help myself
by living all these lives
nine at once or ninety
so that death finds me at all times
and on all sides exposed,
unfortressed, undefended,
inviolable, vulnerable, alive.

Song

O when I was a dirty little virgin
I'd sit and pick my scabby knees
and dream about some man of thirty
and doing nothing did what I pleased.

A woman gets and is begotten on,
have and receive is feminine for live.
I knew it, I knew it even then:
what after all did I have to give?

A flowing cup, a horn of plenty
fulfilled with more than she can hold,
but the milk and honey will be emptied,
emptied out, as she grows old.

More inward than sex or even womb,
inmost in woman is the girl intact,
the dirty little virgin who sits and dreams
and has nothing to do with fact.

Tao Song

O slow fish
show me the way
O green weed
grow me the way

The way you go
the way you grow
is the way
indeed

O bright Sun
light me the way
the right way
the one
no one can say

If one can choose it
it is wrong
Sing me the way
O song:

No one can lose it
for long

Invocation

Give me back my language,
let me speak the tongue you taught me.
I will lie the great lies in your honor,
praise you without naming you,
obey the laws of darkness and of metrics.
Only let me speak my language
in your praise, silence of the valleys,
north side of the rivers,
third face averted,
emptiness!
Let me speak my native tongue
and I will sing so loudly
newlyweds and old women
will dance to my singing
and sheep will cease from cropping and machines
will gather round to listen
in cities fallen silent
as a ring of standing stones.
O let me sing the walls down, Mother!

The Mind Is Still

The mind is still. The gallant books of lies
are never quite enough.
Ideas are a whirl of mazy flies
    over the pigs' trough.

Words are my matter. I have chipped one stone
for thirty years and still it is not done,
that image of the thing I cannot see.
I cannot finish it and set it free,
    transformed to energy.

I chip and stutter but I do not sing
the truth, like any bird.
Daily I come to Judgment stammering
    the same half-word.

So what's the matter? I can understand
that stone is heavy in the hand.
Ideas flit like flies above the swill.
I crowd with other pigs to get my fill.
    The mind is still.

The Marrow

There was a word inside a stone.
I tried to pry it clear,
mallet and chisel, pick and gad,
until the stone was dropping blood,
but still I could not hear
the word the stone had said.

I threw it down beside the road
among a thousand stones
and as I turned away it cried
the word aloud within my ear
and the marrow of my bones
heard, and replied.

The Writer to the Dancer

Shifty Lord let me be honest
Let me be honest shifty Lord

Let me go sideways sideways
Let me go sideways shifty Lord
there is doors Lord doors
opening sideways

From The Dancing at Tillai

Middle

When the pure act turns to drygoods
and the endless yearning
to an earned sum,
when payday comes:

the silly sniveling soul
had better run
stark naked to the woods
and dance to the beating drums.

    Turning, turning,
call the dance out, master,
call out the silly soul.
    Curtsy to your partner,
        do-si-do.
Call out the comets, sister,
and dance the Great Year whole.

The only act that is its end
is the stars' burning.
Swing your partner round and round,
    turning, turning.

At Three Rivers, April '80

A tree that blossoms in the wilderness
in some April beyond history
and farther west than all the pioneers
is in no way less
though there be none to bless
and no woman stand in tears
under the whitening flowers.

Only the tears were ours.

Slick Rock Creek, September

My skin
touches the wind.

A lacewing fly touches my hand.
I speak too slow
                for her to understand.

Rock's warm under my hand.
It speaks too slow
                for me to understand.

I drink sunlit water.

Winter Downs

for Barbara

Eyes look at you.
Thorns catch at you.
Heart starts and bleats.

The looks are rocks
white-ringed with chalk,
flint fish-eyes of old seas,
sheep's flint-dark gaze.

Chalk is sheep-white.
Clouds take shape
and quiet of sheep.
Thorn's hands hold stolen fleece.
The stones sleep open-eyed.

Keep watch. Be not afraid.

Peak

How long to climb the mountain?

Forty years. The native guides
are dark, small, brave, evasive.
They cannot be bribed.

Would you advise
the North Face?

           All the faces
frown, so choose. The travelers describe
their traveling, not yours.
Footholds don't last in ice.
Read rocks, their word endures.

And at the top?
               You stop.

They say that you can see
the Town.
    I don't know.
You look down. It's strange
not to be looking up, hard to be sure
just what it is you're seeing.
Some say the Town, others perceive
a farther range. The guides turn back.
Shoulder your pack, put on your coat.
From here on down no track,

no goal, no way, no ways.
In the immense downward of the evening
there may be far within the golden haze
a motion or a glittering: waves,
towers, heights? remote, remote.
The language of the rocks has changed.
I knew once what it meant.

How long is the descent?

The Child on the Shore

Wind, wind, give me back my feather
Sea, sea, give me back my ring
Death, death, give me back my mother
    So that she can hear me sing

Song, song, go and tell my daughter
Tell her that I wear the ring
Say I fly upon the feather
    Fallen from the falcon's wing

Tui

Life is easy for the youngest daughter.
Her name is Tui, little fish in water.
Her brothers tease and praise her.
She is obstinate and lazy
and quick-hearted. She and her mother
talk for hours together.
"I'm going to catch that minnow,"
her father says, "and fry it in a pan
with parsley." She laughs, she darts away.
Her life is easy and her name means Joy.

From Wild Oats and Fireweed *(1980–1987)*

Wild Oats and Fireweed

I dream of you,
I dream of you jumping,
Rabbit, jackrabbit, and quail.

A foolish daughter of immigrants,
prodigal, hybrid,
I was promiscuous.

The weed beside the road
casts its seed wide.

It furthers to cross the great water.

Old, I am only
this dirt, returning
to this ground,
a sharecropper.
O my America! my new-found-land!

The wild oats,
even, are foreign.

Weed and worthless foolsgold of the hills
of my childhood, my California,
let me be worthy
the stone: the pollen:
the word spoken where the water rises:

the four colors of earth.
Let me in life hold
and pass before dying
the pouch of the silent things
of the six directions.
Let me dream,
let me dream of you jumping,
rabbit, jackrabbit, and quail.

The red weed by roadsides
flowers, in clearcuts and burns
and the wastes of St. Helens,
a tall, feathered dancer
casting its ash-seeds.

O my America!
From the north ice, the raven's,
through the coyote-colored lands
and the Sun's heights and empires
to the south ice, the fireland,
they stand, the Rockies, Andes,
backbone of the black vulture
nailed to the barnside,
the vermin, the varmint.

My body is nail
and condor.
My breath is bullet
and feather.

I return, I turn, I turn in place.
I am my inheritance.

On the edge of the mountain a cloud hangs
and my heart
my heart
my heart hangs with it.

Late I have learned the last direction.
May I before death
learn some words of my language.

From In the Red Zone: Mount St. Helens, October 1981

To Walk In Here

To walk in here is to stop pretending.

What's real? Grey dust,
    a dead forest.
Entropy moves quickly to its end.
O desolation!
        What's real?
    says the fireweed lightly casting
    its words upon the wind.

To walk in here is to stop pretending
that what we do matters
all that much. Less in the long run
than the fireweed, to the others.

To ourselves we matter
terribly.

That there will be summer
ever
is the responsibility of others
more careful than ourselves.

They do not look us in the face.

The gulfs of air
are full of blowing rain
between us and the crater,

the small, cold rain of autumn.

Eternal Life sits on the leaf
cleaning green wings with tiny legs.
Eternal Life, a four-horned turd,
winds graceful up the hemlock stalk.
Eternal Life with garnet facet eyes
alights and realights from blade to blade
of the Eternal Life that grows from every root.
    And still we rant of heaven
and breathe it in and still spit poison out.
The snake is innocent and wise: we spurn
Eternal Life beneath our heel.
I pray you, grass, return, erase.
I pray you, slug and worm,
you who can eat hemlock, can you stomach us?
I pray you, air, forgive us.
I pray you, life, forget—
                Stop.
There is a finger on my lips
no longer than a beetle's leg.
A little worm is in my daughter's womb
who innocent and wise
stops me and will not let me prophesy.
Cassandra must be virgin,
as all women are, this much I've lived to learn,
but in man's definition; she must speak
to men in the language of men with a man's tongue,
and then they will not hear her
because they understand her.
But I talk now in the thick tongue of a woman

to an unborn baby.
In that language is no prophecy.
Twice I bore death, thrice I bore life,
I know this language well.
I know how you learn it.
  Baby, baby, maybe to be born,
little one, fear nothing.
You can hear me, child.
Sleep and be born,
the morning will come,
the grass grows green, the small flies sing,
welcome here and never fear.
You are the Life Eternal,
baby, baby, maybe to be born.
Sweet summer's daughter's child of winter,
come to her, come to me, come.

For the New House

May this house be full of kitchen smells
and shadows and toys and nests of mice
and roars of rage and waterfalls of tears
and deep sexual silences and sounds
of mysterious origin never explained
and troves and keepsakes and a lot of junk
and a flowing like a warm wind only slower
blowing the leaves of trees and books and the fish-years
of a child's life silvery flickering
quick, quick, in the slow incessant gust
that billows out the curtains for a moment
all those years from now, ago.
May the sills and doorframes
be in blessing blest at every passing.
May the roof but not the rooms know rain.
May the windows know clearly
the branch and flower of the apple tree.
And may you be in this house
as the music is in the instrument.

The Maenads

Somewhere I read
that when they finally staggered off the mountain
into some strange town, past drunk,
hoarse, half naked, blear-eyed,
blood dried under broken nails
and across young thighs,
but still jeering and joking, still trying
to dance, lurching and yelling, but falling
dead asleep by the market stalls,
sprawled helpless, flat out, then
middle-aged women,
respectable housewives,
would come and stand nightlong in the agora
silent
together
as ewes and cows in the night fields,
guarding, watching them
as their mothers
watched over them.
And no man
dared
that fierce decorum.

Inventory

The map of the tributaries of the Amazon
in blue, on the right thigh;
lesser river systems
on the lower left leg.
Extremities far more extreme:
knobbed, wired, bent, and multiknuckled.
Some dun cloud
drifts across the color of the eye,
that aged nestling in its baggy nest,
still avid, still insatiable.
Replacement of cheek by jowl,
of curve by hook or crook.
Moles, warts, wenlets, cancerlings,
a distressed finish, constellations,
here the Twins, there the Cluster,
fleshy Pleiades
coming out thick at evening of the skin,
pied beauty—there is none
that hath not some Strangeness in the Proportion.
So the columnar what was waist
sockets to the cushioned pediment
of hips and buttocks. Parts are missing. Scars
lie smiling soft and small among the folds
and hillocks of that broad countryside.
Oh, have I not my rivers and my stars,
my wrinkled ranges in the Western sun?
Oh, have I not my Strangeness?
I am this continent,
and still explore and find no boundary,

for the far sandy beaches of my mind
where soft vast waves and winds erase
the words, the faces—this is still
endless, this is endless still.
I am that wind, that ocean.

A Meditation on a Marriage

From my California, my great land
of gold and complications, wilderness,
enormous cities built on faults,
austere, bizarre, and inexhaustible
vineyards, valleys crowded with visions,

to your Georgia of red dirt
farms, where trees are all one green,
a bony piny sandy silence,
your Georgia of slow rivers, graves,
islands, that quiet place,

how could I come with all my California?

I see them come with open hands,
transparent, sharing everything,
giving and cleaving, nothing kept,
the emigrants that leave their motherland
for love and never look behind.

But if I would how could I give you
California? And I have to live
there, working the creeks my veins for gold.
Or you, could you leave Georgia,
leaving your bones behind,
and give me more than silence?

So we have made these no-one's-lands
by meeting where we never know

when we shall meet or not,
like spies or pioneers,
telling the news in low voices
down in the willow coulees
in a grey evening, inland.

We met at sea, we married
in a foreign language: what wonder
if we cross a continent on foot
each time to find each other
at secret borders, bringing
of all my streams and darknesses of gold
and your deep graves and islands
a feather
a flake of mica
a willow leaf
that is our country,
ours alone.

The Crown of Laurel

He liked to feel my fingers in his hair.
So he pulled them off me, wove a wreath of them,
and wears it at parades and contests,
my dying fingers with their kitchen smell
interlocked around his sunny curls.
Sometimes he rests on me a while.
Aside from that, he seems to have lost interest.

It wasn't to preserve my virtue that I ran!
What's a nymph like me
to do with something that belongs to men?
It's just I wasn't in the mood.
And he didn't care. It scared me.

The little goatleg boys can't even talk,
but still they wait till they can smell you feel
like humping with a goatleg in the woods,
rolling and scratching and laughing — they can laugh! —
poor little hairycocks, I miss them.

When we were tired of that kind of thing
my sister nymphs and I would lie around
and talk, and tease, and stroke, and chase, and stretch
out panting for another talk, and sleep
in the warm shadows side by side
under the leaves, and all was as we pleased.

And then the mortal hunters of the deer,
the poachers, the deciduous shepherd boys:
they'd stop and gape and stare with owly eyes,
not even hoping, even when I smiled.
New every spring, like daffodils, those boys.

But once for forty years I met one man
up on the sheep-cropped hills of Arcady.
I kissed his wrinkles, the ravines of time
I cannot enter, gazing in his eyes, whose dark

dimmed and deepened, seeing less always, till he died.
I came to his burial. Among the villagers
I walked behind his grey-haired wife.
She could have been Time's wife, my grandmother.

And then there were my brothers of the streams,
O my river-lovers, with their silver tongues,
so sweet to thirst! the cool, prolonged delight
of a river moving in me, of his flow and flow and flow!
They send to my roots their kindness, even now,
and slowly I drink it from my mother's hands.

So that was all I knew, until he came
hard, bright, burning, dry, intent:
one will, instead of wantings meeting:
no center but himself, the Sun. A god
is like that, I suppose; he has to be.
But then, I never asked to meet a god,

let alone make love with one. Why did he think
I wanted to? And when I told him no,
what harm did he think it did him?
It can't be hard to find a girl agape
to love a big blond blue-eyed god.
He said so, said, "You're all alike."
He's seen us all; he knows. So, why me?

I guess that maybe it was time for me
to give up going naked, and get dressed.
And it took a god to make me do it.
Mother never could. So I put on
my brown, ribbed stockings, and my underwear
of silky cambium, and my green dress.
And I became my clothing, being what I wear.

I run no more; the winds dance me.
My sister, seamstress, sovereign comes
up from the dark below the roots
to mend my clothes in April. And I stand
in my green patience in the winter rains.

He honors me, he says, to wear
my fingers turning brown and brittle, clenched
in the bright hair of his head. He sings.

My silence crowns the song.

The Pacific Slope

I love that, "the Pacific Slope," I see
snowtiger cloudy granite of the Sierras
and silver scree of the Cascades, vast sweeps
and westward slidings down to wild oats and oaks
in valleys, cresting to the Coast Range, then
tangled in ceanothus and salal, and last
fast falling off cliff, down dune, slopes
sweet in fog and sunlight to the sea.

Riding the "Coast Starlight"

I saw white pelicans rise
from the waters of morning
in the wide valley, going.
I saw trees white with snow
rise silent from clouds
in the deep mountains, returning.
Heavy, noble, solemn the gesture
of the wings, the branches,
a white writing on destruction.

Sleeping with Cats

In smoothness of darkness are
warm lumps of silence.
There are no species.
Purring recurs.

Waking: Two Poems

I

Drifting on the April river
of the dark, sweet winds
broken by birdsong rapids,
I am borne to daylight.

II

In the grey cocoon of light the mind
finds metamorphosis,
makes from the wreck of what she was
the wings of what she is.

The Vigil for Ben Linder

killed in 1986 by "contras" while working as an engineer in a volunteer group bringing electric power to villages in Nicaragua

This rain among the candle flames
under the heavy
end of April evening
falls so softly on us
listening
that it dissolves us
like salt.

A child frets.
The grieving over names.
The same anger.
There are still far countries.

Mayday! they signal,
it's sinking, crashing, it's going
down now! Mayday!
But it used to mean
you went into the garden
early, that first morning,
to make a posy
for a neighbor's door,
or boldly offered—
"These are for your daughter!"—

laughing, because she wasn't up yet.
They were maybe twelve years old.
Afterwards they went to different schools.

The bringing of light
is no simple matter.
The offering of flowers
is a work of generations.

Young men are scattered
like salt on a dry ground.
Not theirs, not theirs
but ours
the brave children
who must learn the rules.

To bring light
to flower in a dark country
takes experts in illumination,
engineers of radiance.

Taken, taken and broken.

We are dim circles flickering
at nightfall in April in the rain
that quickens the odor of flowering trees
and the odor of stone.
Over us
is a dark government.

Circles of burning flames, of flowers,
of children learning light.
Circles of rain on stone and skin.
Turning and returning in shaken silence,
broken, unbroken.
Sorrow is the home country.

The Queen of Spain, Grown Old and Mad, Writes to the Daughter She Imagines She Had by Christopher Columbus

Most beautiful,
I disclaim you.
You are not my new found land
nor my Hesperides
nor my America.
You are not mine
and I do not name you.
   I tear up the map
of the world of you
that had your rivers
in the wrong places,
imaginary mountains,
false passes leading my expeditions
to quicksands,
cannibals, jaguars.
   Most truthful,
I disown you.
I do not own you.
Truly I have never known you.
   When you tell me
who you are
I will call you by that name.
When you tell me
where you are
my compass will point there.
When you tell me
of your prairies, your sierras,
I will see them in the blue air

above the western sea.
    O golden Peru,
treasure never mine,
most beautiful, most true!
Between us
is neither forgiveness
nor reparation
but only the sea waves, the sea wind.
    If ever you send
across the sea,
bells will be rung
in the old towers
and the Te Deum sung.
Crowned, jeweled, furred,
I will come forward:
Tell me, my Lord Ambassadors!
From the New World
what word, what word?

Mother of my granddaughter,
listen to my song:
A mother can't do right,
a daughter can't be wrong.

I have no claim whatever
on amnesty from you;
nor will she forgive you
for anything you do.

So are we knit together
by force of opposites,
the daughter that unravels
the skein the mother knits.

One must be divided
so that one be whole,
and this is the duplicity
alleged of woman's soul.

To be that heavy mother
who weighs in every thing
is to be the daughter
whose footstep is the Spring.

Granddaughter of my mother,
listen to my song:
Nothing you do will ever be right,
nothing you do is wrong.

The Hard Dancing

Dancing on the sun is hard,
it burns your feet, you have to leap
higher and higher into the dark,
until you somersault to sleep.
The mountains of the sun are steep,
rising to shadow at the crown,
the valleys of the sun are deep
and ever brighter deeper down.

From No Boats *(chapbook, 1991)*

From "McKenzie Voices"

for Ruth and Judith

There is a river above the river,
like the dreaming or the breathing of the river.
Only as the sun rises over the cedars
can you see the spirit river flowing slowly,
but listen as you will, you will not hear it.

At Cannon Beach

The day goes out grey
with the low tide,
still, cold: twilight
colorless under cloud.
I have not said a word
aloud all day.
Sounds cease.
Silence, solitude,
peace.

The Aching Air

Where the most beautiful
horsechestnut held up deep branches
in a cathedral
full of wings and voices
and a golden light,
and the tall, rose-white flowers
smelled like the bread of heaven,
and eyes praised upraised,
being blest by seeing:
where the tree was
the air's empty.

The insatiable vacuum
of a mean fear
in envy of that strength,
that lively age,
sucked there.
Destruction, the old man raged,
give me destruction!
And he got what he wanted.

Trees are so dirty,
the lady said.
The birds make the car
so dirty. All fall
I have to sweep the sidewalk.

Five fingers
has the chestnut hand,
loosely holding
candles, conkers,
sunlight, twilight,
and letting them fall.

They cut off the giant branches
first, then sawed rounds
from the top down the trunk
to the stump. Can't let it fall.
So saw off the fingers,
then wrists and ankles,
then knees and elbows,
then hips and shoulders,
so that nobody
gets hurt.

Then poison the enormous
stump, that keeps on trying
to send up shoots.
Hack at the roots
and finally pull it
like a huge tooth.

The broken wood
was sweet and white.
People kept coming by,

slowing down in cars,
stopping walking, to stare.
Nothing there.

No fall,
all fall.
All clean.
All bare.
Only the tall,
tree-shaped, empty,
aching air.

Read at the Award Dinner, May 1996

Beware when you honor an artist.
You are praising danger.
You are holding out your hand
to the dead and the unborn.
You are counting on what cannot be counted.

The poet's measures serve anarchic joy.
The story-teller tells one story: freedom.

Above all beware of honoring women artists.
For the housewife will fill the house with lions
and in with the grandmother
come bears, wild horses, great horned owls, coyotes.

Hexagram 45

Gather round me all my words!
Aunty Change has said to gather,
said the Emperor comes to the palace.
Come closer to me, closer!
Arrange yourselves in order,
peasants, merchants, artisans, lords,
common nouns and working verbs,
beautiful adjectives, names of glory.
Assume your syntax, raise your swords,
shouting, roaring, inventing meanings.
Save me from the silent demons.
Where there's blue shout red! red!
Where there's end make story, story.

When there aren't any

and when nothing beats,
no crow just past the edge of sight
heavily seeking, no echo dogging
the syllable, no rim of light
around the sound, no feet
dancing, what do you do?

Suck the mud and wait.

Mudsucker mudsucker seeking to say
what? say what? is it right
to say what's left to say? whose right?

O I have earned my urn, and sixty years
of spading at my grave has dug it whole enough
for all my little partialities.

World,
you interpenetrate my mesh. The tendriled gods
still climb my spine, stars are my tears,
birds wing my feet and lions lick my hair,
but the net of mankind wears so thin
that the old soul falls through, slick fish,
cynic butterfly, shadow of a crow.
What shall I say in the speech
that tears the web to shreds,

the tongue of my killing people?
Can singing heal the sea?

I will suck sand, talk salt.
I will fear silence. Grandmother!
Teach me the weaving
and the words to be said.

Rodmell

When we walked in the garden of love
lovers were walking there
alone, in couples, in threes
under the apple trees in the uncertain air.

Nobody was there but lovers
silently seeking what they wanted,
the river where she set down her burden
near the garden he planted.

Wind washes over the long light downs.
By her house walk those who love her.
She became the river and was burned to ashes
and there is no earth above her.

For Gabriela Mistral

En el Valle de Elqui, ceñido
de cien montañas o de más . . .

Forty years beyond her mortal years
she came back to me, to our Pacific,
she came here, she
who sank the meek and blinded saint
and the grim men from Spain
in the glory of the lord of angels
and a gust of the craziest wind.
She stood on this northern shore
where gulls whirled like torn paper
and said in the language that I spoke
before I spoke words, "Come!"

"Come!" she said, standing
heavy-bodied and rough-voiced,
deep-breasted as the hills:
"I came north, but you didn't know me.
I've gone home now to the valley
encircled by a hundred mountains,
a hundred mountains, maybe more.
You must come and you must learn
my language."

   If I walk south
with the ocean always on my right
and the mountains on my left,
swimming the mouths of the rivers,

the estuaries and the great canal,
if I walk from high tide to low tide
and full moon to new moon, south,
and from equinox to solstice, south,
across the equator in a dream of volcanoes,
if I walk through all the Tropics
past bays of amethyst and bays of jade
from April spring to April autumn, south,
and cross the deserts of niter and asbestos
with the sea silver on my right
and a hundred mountains on my left,
a hundred mountains, maybe more,
I will come to the valley.

If I walk all the way, my poet,
if I can walk all the way,
I will come to you.
And I will speak your language.

Hexagram 49

para mi Diana

How could I not love her? She
wants what cannot be
owned, or known, or gone;
the way she seeks to find
is the other one; the me
she hunts does not exist, her
"baby, mother, friend, sister,"
purer, stronger than ever I
or woman was, her "interlocutor
in the secret rivers of the mind."

She transforms all to forest.
She shames the owning, knowing,
gaining of an end, she shines
incandescent, without compromise.
All that was and will be lost
is golden in the puma's eyes.

The fire in the secret river.
How could I not love her?

Infinitive

We make too much history.

With or without us
there will be the silence
and the rocks and the far shining.

But what we need to be
is, oh, the small talk of swallows
in evening over
dull water under willows.

To be we need to know the river
holds the salmon and the ocean
holds the whales as lightly
as the body holds the soul
in the present tense, in the present tense.

"The scarcity of rhinos"
(unimaginably)
"in this region
is such that individuals
only are known."
They run from the camera. The scarcity
of imagination, the paucity
of rhinos, the poverty
of cities, the scarcity
of probity, are probably
connected.
The rhinos of invention
are poorer than the individuals
in the cities of the poverty
of the imagination of the politicians
of paucity.

O rhinoceroses of unimaginable real horns
of plenty on savannahs of enormous
vegetables and animals and connections!

Individuals make moving pictures
of the extinction of 300 species
daily and individually
watch them running
into the distances
of all the plenty
of the indivisible world.

The horn of the rhinoceros
finely divided is imagined
to assure longevity
to the human
individual.

O awkward and shortsighted
and short-lived rhinoceros,
bearing the living
horn, the one true one!
Where?

FIELD BURNING DEBATED, SALMON FATE DISCUSSED.

We are the desert god.
His left hand plucks from the burning
what his right hand burns.

The farmer in the photo holds a stalk of fescue:
"To you people it's just grass.
To me it's money."
In autumn it goes up in smoke,
a fitting sacrifice.

The nations of the salmon
return upriver to the festival
of the nations of the desert,
leap, and become money in midair.
There is no festival.

The god debates fate
while with his hands he feeds his mouth,
eating the fingers one by one.

Morning Service

So still so sunny and so Sunday
is this early day,
what's done needs to be quiet:
a white butterfly
by the red fuses of the fuchsias.

The sounds are the sea
that only breaks its silence
meeting other elements,
and a hummingbird saying tek!
tek! as it attacks the fuchsias.

Nothing else says anything.
I am trying to be still.
This is the church I go to
to hear the hymns and prayers
and see the light.

Late Dusk

The sky is rose quartz amethyst
over dark hill dark trees dark roof.
Say dark so long it has no meaning.
Say I would be farther west.
Say I am not far enough.
Say the light is beautiful, failing.

A Blue Moon: June 30

Cold north blows through hot sun.
I seek to be by doing things.
The wind does the wind; the sun is one;
I am the center of many rings,

a sphere enclosed in other spheres,
an absence in a solitude.
The sun is round, as round as years.
Is my hunger all my food?

A blue moon will rise tonight
as the sun sets across the wind.
I have done. I have done right.
Now let my being begin and sing.

The sun turns south; the wind is cold.
North and silence eat the old.

Repulse Monkey

How I seek and seek through fear
a balance where I will be whole,
yet in scattered months of years
hide the fragments of my soul.

How I fear and fear to find
which is the year, the month, the week,
so that each movement of my mind
turns me away from what I seek,

that balance point, that backward chance,
the avoided center of the dance.

"Will the Circle Be Unbroken?"

No, when they went, we said goodbye.

But why do we break through into love
to be instantly and constantly forsaken?
Is it a mere failure of perception
that makes the whole seem broken?

No, when I go, goodbye, I'm gone.

But still sometimes it seems like
the Grandmother Dance at the powwow,
the circling, the singing, and the endless drumming,
the intent faces passing, coming past, coming round.

Incredible Good Fortune

O California, dark, shaken, broken hills,
bright fog reaching over the beaches,
madrone and diggerpine and Valley oak,
I'm your dryhearted daughter.
I listened when the earthquake spoke
and learned what the quail teaches.
The stony bed the rain of winter fills
waited all year for the water.

April in San Jose

In a city where men shout across the streets
Shit Shit   God bless you lady   ay Miguel
bark wordless pain like dogs,
roar rage in one dark syllable,
or stand and beat an oak tree with their fists,
or walk ten feet of driveway back and forth
in boots and Nazi cap and steel chains,
or sit and shiver, silent, in the sun,

I steer among the wrecks, the reefs,

through poppies, roses, red valerian,
passionflower, trumpet vine,
camellia, dogwood, foam of plum and pear,
mock orange and true orange,
gold of the Hesperides,
sweetness of freesias, garlands, wreaths
of red and yellow, white and green,
dark fragrance of eucalyptus,
glitter and rustle of inordinate palms.

Through the mockingbird morning
I make my way bewildered,
in the city of ruined men
in the valley of the ghosts of orchards
in the broken heart of California
in the nation of addiction
in the kindest month.

Mount Rainier from Amtrak

We steal on steel through vague terrains
of sheds and fences, weeds and waste.
Over the jumbled, trashy plains

the mountain lifts its owl-skull face,
immensely silent, blind with sun,
inhabitant of another space,

alien to things that run
on tracks and roads, to scurfs of roofs,
crisscrossing wires, confusion:

enormous and indifferent proof
to passing souls in passing trains
that what can bless us stands aloof.

The Cactus Wren

(Joshua Tree National Park)

In this great silence, to sit still
and listen till I hear the wren
is to draw free from wish and will.
    She flits to perch; her slender bill
spouts a thin jet of music; then
in the great silence she falls still.
    Wind nods the short-stemmed flowers that fill
the sandy wash. She sings again
her song devoid of wish or will.
    The hummingbird's quick drum and thrill
is gone just as I hear it, when
in this great silence all holds still.
    The granite sand, the barren hill,
the dry, vast, rigorous terrain
answer no human wish or will.
    Again, the small quicksilver trill
that has no messages for men.
In the great silence she sings still
of pure need free from wish or will.

The Old Lady

I have dreed my dree, I have wooed my wyrd,
and now I shall grow a five-foot beard
and braid it into tiny braids
and wander where the webfoot wades
among the water's shining blades.
I will fear nothing I have feared.
I'm the queen of spades, the jack of trades,
braiding my knives into my beard.

Why should I know what I have known?
Once was enough to make it my own.
The things I got I will forget.
I'll knot my beard into a net
and cast the net and catch a fish
who will ungrant my every wish
and leave me nothing but a stone
on the riverbed alone,
leave me nothing but a rock
where the feet of herons walk.

The Forsaken Shepherdess

I love to sit beside the stream
that runs so fast and fiery,
setting the forest trees aflame
with the joy of its desiring.

I watch the fishes of the stream,
the blinding trout, the blazing carp,
and hear its music go and come,
plucking the incandescent harp.

I'll sit beside the lava stream
as my lambs leap and gambol
like molten clouds at sunset time,
flocking crimson, fleeting nimble.

I'll pipe my tune of joy and shame,
a simple shepherdess alone,
while slower, blacker runs the stream
and all the lowlands turn to stone.

Notes from a Cruise

Antigua: The Silence of the Mountain

A long, long line slants up the sky,
half seen half guessed: through milky haze
it draws the eye and draws the eye
higher and higher still, amazed
that silent earth can raise so high
a pure geometry of praise.
But churches bowed and towers broke
the last time the volcano spoke.

Pelicans

They're awkward, angular, abstruse,
the great beak on a head so narrow,
a kind of weird Jurassic goose
lurching into the modern era.
But the blue arc of sky lets loose —
look, now! — the brown, unerring arrow!
And see how beautiful, how grave,
the steady wings along the wave.

Talk Shows

In rush and gush of wordy juice
the torrents of our talking run,
I say to you, he says to them,
the sap that swells the human stem.

Listen, listen, a lesser voice,
a whisper of the wind on stone
along the river's drouth-white bed,
the shadow of the word unsaid.

Here, There, at the Marsh

The papers are full of war and
my head is full of the anguish of battles
and ruin of ancient cities

In the rainy light a great blue heron
lifts and flies above the brown cattails
heavy, tender, and pitiless

American Wars

Like the topaz in the toad's head
the comfort in the terrible histories
was up front, easy to find:
Once upon a time in a kingdom far away.

Even to the dreadful now of news
we listened comforted
by far time-zones, languages we didn't speak,
the wide, forgetful oceans.

Today, no comfort but the jewel courage.
The war is ours, now, here, it is our republic
facing its own betraying terror.
And how we tell the story is forever after.

The Lost Explorer

They were all known and named, the rivers of his North:
Columbia, Wakiakum, Cathlamet, Deep:
clear, dark, strong-running rivers of the truth.

So he set out, how many years ago, to seek
across uncharted ranges of the mind, beyond
the maps and histories, for rivers no one knows,
that leap from undiscovered springs into the sun.
He found and followed the bright, nameless streams; he found,
past all the lonely plains, the sea to which they run.

He wanders aimless now along the echoing beach
of that long coast outside the compass rose,
and glimpsing farther islands he will never reach,
names their imagined rivers with the names of home:
Cathlamet and Columbia; the Deep; Wakiakum.

Ille

Ride beside me,
sleep beside me,
brother ghost
never born.
Be my guide
when I'm lost
and alone.
From your distance
bring me close
to the bone.
Ride with me where I must go.
Dream in me what I must see.
Be what I cannot be.
Be almost me,
brother ghost.
Let me be other,
almost brother.
Set me free.
Ride beside me.
Sleep with me.

Invocation

O silence, my love silence,
I have feared you: my tongue
has rattled on my teeth
dreading to be dumb so long
when I am done with breath.
    And I have needed prattle,
kind blather, and the come and go
of voices, human voices,
the sky whose moon you are,
the ground whose flower.
    But I beseech you come
now, my love silence, O
reward and freedom, balance
beyond choices, in whom alone is heard
the meditation of the twilight bird
and the never to be spoken word.

Dance Song

This breath is not any other breath.
Not breathed before, not breathed again.
In a now without a then
it interleaves me with my death.

So for a moment I am free.
Once I breathe, and only once.
Wind blows me and I dance,
willow leaf on willow tree.

English

I love my native language
the lovely viola
the great advantage

a mouthful of pebbles
a welling of water
crashbangs   faint echoes

the word if you can find it
for what is and
what is beyond it

Taking Courage

I will build a hardiness
    of counted syllables,
asylum for the coward heart
    that stammers out my hours,
an armature of resonance,
    a scaffolding of spell,
where it can learn to keep the time
    and bid what comes come well.

A Request

Should my tongue be tied by stroke
listen to me as if I spoke

and said to you, "My dear, my friend,
stay here a while and take my hand;

my voice is hindered by this clot,
but silence says what I cannot,

and you can answer as you please
such undemanding words as these.

Or let our conversation be
a mute and patient amity,

sitting, all the words bygone,
like a stone beside a stone.

It takes a while to learn to talk
the long language of the rock."

For Naomi

My mother-body held me tight.
I sucked the flowing world from her,
the sweet air, the warm light,
and she sang sleep to me at night.

There's no more comfort in her breast
and only distance in her arms.
She no longer holds me close.
"Go on," she sings now, "little ghost."

Learning Latin in Old Age

I feel so foolish sitting translating Vergil,
the voices of ancient imaginary shepherds,
in a silent house in Georgia, listening
for that human sweetness but afraid,
gathering griefs, my flock of goats
dry-uddered and with evil eyes, around me,
seeking the word that will turn them to eagles
or dry leaves to fly off, begone, the word
not even Vergil knew, who died with his work unfinished.

Futurology

I cannot break free from these iron stars.
I want the raspberry paw-pads of the fox,
but here are only claws, the Crab, the Scorpion,
great shining signs that slide across the sky.

I want the wisdom ignorant of wars
and the soft key that opens all the locks.
I want the touch of fur, the slant of sun
deep in a golden, slotted, changing eye.

O let there be no signs! Let fall the bars,
and walls be moss-grown, scattered rocks.
Let all the evil we have done be done
and minds lie still as sunlit meadows lie.

II

Life Sciences
New Poems, 2006–2010

I. Socioesthetics

Distance

If we refuse the notion of away,
could we relearn the truth of far?
We deny distance, busy filling it
with what we throw out of the car,
paving the house of Shiva with our shit,
scumming Poseidon's silver hair with tar,
fouling the quail's nest. Away is where
we live, and here is where we are,
a long distance from the nearest star.

Pretty Things

In Chinatown in 1938
a bowl-plate of cheap porcelain, "peasant ware,"
they called it, painted by a swift sure hand
with lively leaves and bright blob-flowers, cost
twenty-five cents. I still have six of them.

The girls, in 1965, would help me steer
the stroller to the Five and Ten, and each,
after some intense pondering, would choose
a single plastic flower. A dime apiece.
I have it still, a bouquet long in gathering.

Getting and spending—yes, I know. But things,
cheap little pretty things, bought with joy
and kept because of it, don't they contain
an immaterial radiance, maybe finally
the flicker of immortality called soul?

You see such things in bins at the Goodwill.
Sad grey bits of wreckage from a flood.
Mine will just be stuff the kids
have to dispose of. Or the Chinese plates
might be quite valuable, in money. But that

was never what that flickering radiance was.

In England in the Fifties

Over the cities and villages hovering
coal smoke drew curtains, gauze-veils of darkness
even in daylight, blackening windowsills,
ledges and cornices, drifting in tiny bituminous
particles into the lungs. Still the remembered
scent of those hearthfires haunts me,
rich with nostalgia. Resinous fragrance of forests
unthinkably ancient, incense shrunk to a black rock
buried and hidden deep, deep for eons:
dug out with heart-killing labor, laid on a hearthstone,
lighted. Myrrh on an ignorant altar. Arson of centuries.
Forest after forest unclosed all its complex, sweet darkness,
curled up into the wind, and was gone where the wind went.

The City of the Plain

What can I make it a metaphor for? This is transgression
made concrete and asphalt and 30-foot palms of aluminum.
This is the Gonetoofar. The Great Slot. A 3-D spectacular:
Moses meets Bambi in the technicolooliah desert yes Lord!
where pyramids tangle with hiltons, 4/5-size towers of eiffel
or possibly lego crouch under condos and blu-blu skies scraped
clean of all cloud, except for the yellowish forest-fire
smoke from the mountains up yonder, actual mountains, 5/5-size,
burning, but nobody's worried. Arable plains, or the lowlands,
my Spanish dictionary says it means, but not to the lady who
    crouches
hour after hour after hour in front of the videopoker game
inhaling the yellowish smoke of her camels burning, but
nobody's worried, and not to the lady who poledances,
and not to the lady who lugs in the bucket and mops.
No; maybe to her, once. Not any more though. Lasvegas
are not any more in a language, is not what it says it is, has
nothing to mean. After lasvegas you have to go into the desert
for a long, for a long, for a long time. Years. Generations.

> *Envoi: to Lot's Wife*
> Salty lady dry your tears
> nothing worth your sorrow
> Salty lady don't look back
> don't look back tomorrow

Watching the Fractal Set

Candidates are hacked into
small bloodless morsels and deepfried
in steroids and the weather will occur while
skyscrapers and redwoods skip about
in earnest spectacles on a nose
two seconds long at most and once again
the Jesus man the zircon bargains scores
of ballgames and the round black ears
while people laugh who are not there or dead
and if you zoom up it seems larger yet
is the same size exactly or zoom down
and it seems tee-tiny but no change in size exactly
all the same the weather Jesus steroids zircons
candidates dead children laughing and
the awful round black ears with round black ears on them
with round black ears on them: the Mouse of Mandelbrot.

The Mistake

The great grey navies wait
on the will of no admiral
but folly and fate.
Men think they make their wars.
They learn their mistake
too hard, too late.

The Next War

It will take place,
it will take time,
it will take life,
and waste them.

The Crest

We who've lived at the top of the crest
of the great wave of owning,
did we really think the wave would never break
and we wouldn't end up drowning?

Soldiers

When I was young, the soldiers filled
    The streets with khaki brown,
And sailors too in white and blue,
    The glory of my town.

My elder brothers all had gone
    To wear a uniform.
I feared for them, but never feared
    They would do any harm.

I knew them brave and kind, I knew
    Them good, and nothing more.
How should a child conceive the wrong
    That is the soul of war?

None of them killed, and none was killed.
    And when their job was done
In hope and pride we welcomed them
    And said the war was won.

When I had children of my own,
    Soldiers were dressed like clowns
In camouflage, and no parades
    Went thumping through the towns.

No, it was we who marched instead,
    And we who beat the drum:

Women and old men, motley, wild,
    All shouting, "Bring them home!"

They brought them home; some were alive,
    But all had come to grief.
And silence met each one and shame
    As for a coward or thief.

We failed them, in righteousness
    Withdrawing our goodwill
From the blind courage that obeyed
    The blind command to kill.

Yet in all truth they failed us,
    As young men ever have,
Who take the order from old men
    To dig our common grave.

So now my children's children see
    Their brothers in the mud,
And tortured prisoners, and streets
    A marsh of human blood.

And it will be in years to come
    As in the years before:
The innocent accept the wrong
    That is the soul of war.

And soldiers still will fill the towns
  In blue or khaki clad,
The brave, the good, who march to kill
  What hope we ever had.

The Curse of the Prophetess

Hear my curse on the nation of Israel and the nation of Palestine.
May the generals of your armies
be little, heavy-burdened donkeys,
and your leaders be patient, old sheep.
May you listen discriminately to your God,
testing the validity of the transmissions,
and heeding not His calls to vengeance.
May your women go bareheaded in His presence
and dance in His temples,
may their wombs be fruitful in girl children.
May your young men take no joy in combat
and your old men be fearful for them, saying,
"Is it right that my son give his life for me?
Am I a better man than he is?
Nay, let him live to be a shepherd
or garage mechanic or professor of ancient languages."
Let the child set down the stone in his hand
and be allowed to learn to make bricks for the building of houses.
Let the mouths that spit forth missiles be stopped with earth.
Let those who give their lives to destroy other lives
be called not heroes but murderers, the disgrace of their people.
Let the day come, let it come now,
when the name warrior will be a name of folly
and the word victory mean a vain thing.
Let the day come, let it come now,
when the wine of intolerant belief is poured out on the sand
so that all may drink from the well they share with their neighbor.
The wine of belief is strong,
driving mad those who drink it:

the wine of hatred is like wormwood:
they who drink it cannot cease drinking.
May the grapes of those vineyards rot on the vines,
may the casks of the vintners burst asunder,
may the vintners be ashamed of their folly.
Then may your peoples go to the well in the marketplace
and draw water together, go out into the desert
seeking the wellsprings, conversing together,
forgetful of old wrongs, remembering kinship.
Let them speak long together of justice
and kneel down then to drink
from the wells and springs that are life in that desert,
praising the giver of the holy waters.
And may this curse be upon you
and your sons and your daughters
to the ninth generation.

Every Land

The holy land is everywhere. —Black Elk

Watch where the branches of the willows bend
See where the waters of the rivers tend
Graves in the rock, cradles in the sand
Every land is the holy land.

Here was the battle to the bitter end
Here's where the enemy killed the friend
Blood on the rock, tears on the sand
Every land is the holy land.

Willow by the water bending in the wind
Bent till it's broken and it cannot stand
Listen to the word the messengers send
Life from the living rock, death in the sand
Every land is the holy land.

The Elders at the Falls

(The Dalles Dam at Celilo Falls on the Columbia, 1957)

I heard this story.
They stood all day with their backs turned.
They stood there just above the river
all the long day with their backs turned
to what was happening.
Like the chorus in ancient tragedies,
not the heroes but the old people
who do not see the battle,
the sacrifice, the murder,
they stood and listened to the messenger,
the voice that tells the story.
The voice they listened to
that had spoken all their lives
and all the lives before them
telling its story, their story, that great voice
Celilo
grew smaller,
became less,
became quieter,
all day, until
at twilight
it was silent.

They turned around then.
They turned and looked at the flat lake of silence.

An Old Yurok Basket

This was made by a most skillful maker:
the ease of the pattern's recurrence is noble,
so is the curve of the whole, and the colors,
the soft yellow-brown and the warm brown.
Yet in the way that it sits, I see something
imperfect, expectant, immediate,
alert, like a bird with its head cocked.
It grew into being. Its stillness remembers
the tug of the living reed-root in the current.
    The humor of pliable, sensitive
fingers is here in the weave of the fernstems,
the even/uneven rhythm of lifework.
And this is what's missing, my heart says, what's missing.

Almost and Always

Almost they were, the amethyst mountains
and the clear, faint holloing of horns
in far forests over the twilight border,
and faded into daylight and the noise of traffic.

Always the half-guessed miraculous line
trembled on the edge of being
in this language, and was almost, and faded
into the expectable ordinary poem.

Lieder Singer

to Ian Bostridge

He stands by the piano, tall and lean
in black, unsmiling. His hands are tense.
Men are unlikely instruments.
A piano too, a strange awkward thing.

He looks out through the audience
waiting for the accompanist to begin
the running rolling subtle Schubert tune.
His gaze changes as he starts to sing.

Now he sees nothing. Is he seen?
Where is he now in these long-drawn laments,
these soft rejoicings in a summer dawn?
Like Echo hidden near the hidden spring,

unbodied into music, he consents
to be nothing but voice, the rest is gone.

Writers

Fortunate those who fill their hands
with stuff of the imagined thing
to shape the cup, the carven bird;
whose fingers strike from key or string
the ringing, single-complex chord,
actual, heard.
              A writer's work
is with the insubstantial word,
the image that can only find
its being in another's mind.
We work with water, with the wind,
we make and hold no thing at all.
All we can ever shape or sing
the tremor of an untouched string,
a shift of shadows on the wall.

After the Fire

for Roger

My tall friend has to stand,
his hands full of ashes.
Every thing he made is gone.
Ungiven. Taken.
His work is smoke.

He has to seek with aching
eyes through the sodden darkness
of ruin and remembrance
to maybe see that clear space
where nothing is forgotten,
nothing forsaken,
nothing familiar.
Where the work waits
patient as ever
for the hand of the maker
to make smoke stay
and ashes blossom.

Lorca's Duende

The duende got into my head
by the back staircase,
a gypsy girl-child dressed in red
with an old man's face.

My bedroom turned bitter cold.
There were banging noises,
loud knockings in between the walls.
Things left their places.

My comb crawled across the bureau,
clicking like castanets.
My grandmother's ivory-backed mirror
cracked itself into bits.

Get out of my head, old child.
Te exorcizo!
Take your tricks and your wild ways
back to Andalusia.

Go home, poltergeist,
and do Spanish damage.
I have my own bad guests
that speak my own bad language.

Meters

I. THE HEROIC COUPLET

I loved, when I was young, the hard, sedate,
controlled iambics, the foot-soldier gait
that swung great armies to their epic goal,
or, slowed, allowed a meditative stroll.
The rhymes might seem, when so exactly struck,
one gate after another shut and stuck;
and yet recurrence reassured, the chime
of an old clock securely keeping time.
And so the strict form gave the fifteen-year-old
(timid and venturesome, withdrawn and bold,
guideless and guileless in the realms of thought)
the steady, stable structure that she sought.
In adolescent tides of fear and hope,
I prized the canny certainties of Pope;
when all I did seemed wrong, it was delight
to hear him say, Whatever is, is right.
With later strength I'd plunge and breast the flow
and heady surge of Shelley and Hugo,
but first I learned to walk with firm intent
the steadfast paths of the Enlightenment.
And in old age, as strength again grows faint,
that poetry of order, wit, restraint,
braces my soul; I honor the clear art,
and let the heroic measure pace my heart.

II. *INGENTI PERCUSSUS AMORE*

And yet forever unfaithful, eternally restless, hard upon eighty,
I sit like the schoolgirl I once was over my Latin lesson,
so that I can read, no, not read, can listen, straining, intense,
to catch a whisper, a breath of the incredible music, the ancient,
remote song, hear the soft voice with its faint country accent
telling how shepherds quarrel for love, how from a chunk of the
    wood
you can grow a whole olive-tree, how the gods harry a good man.
Are you my last poet then, Vergil? last of so many I followed?
None sweeter, none better, never so truthful a guide on the way
that leads into darkness, passing the great tree that shelters
false dreams in clusters like bats under its leaves, to the river
of shadows, and the dim fields where hurt souls gather in silence.

You carried Dante up out of his hell; he turned away from you.
I would ask only to stay with you. You and Lucretius before you
showed me the shores where the foam of the breakers is starlight.
                            Now let me follow
you down, as falling leaves follow the west wind to rest in the earth.

Exegi monumentum aere perennius

Indeed your words were strong and bright as bronze,
    worthy to last forever,
but wisdom itself can't outwear ignorance.
If no one knows the tongue, the poem stands
mute as a crumbling tomb beside a river.

Horace, our house of words is built of clay:
the floods of winter wash it all away.

She Remembers the Famous Poets

Quand vous serez bien vieille, au soir à la chandelle ... — Ronsard
When you are old and grey and full of sleep ... — Yeats

Now I am old and grey and sit alone beside my fire,
I think of lovely boys I knew when I was young and fair.
And some of them wrote poems about my eyes and their desire,
My winsome Irish Willie and my gallant French Pierre.

It makes me smile to think about how we made love, and all
The tender things they told me, as I gaze into the flames
These winter nights; but, Lord! I never can recall
A single word of all they wrote, or even their last names.

II. Botany and Zoology

Two Crow Poems

1. THE WASHINGTON STREET GANG

Crows continually going and coming
call to other crows, caw, cark, talk,
and flit like heavy fragments of cast iron, black,
thrown from this tree to that,
and in that tree or this sit throned
like black, heavy fragments of cast iron, talk,
cark, call, caw to other crows that flit
and sit in a continual coming and going of crows.

2. THE COLOR OF ANARCHY

Crows are the color of anarchy
and close up they're a little scary.
An eye as bright as anything.
Having a pet crow would be
like having Voltaire on a string.

Learning the Name

for Bette

Swainson's thrush, it is! Now I know
who sings that clear arpeggio,
three far notes weaving
into the evening
among leaves
    and shadow,

or at dawn in the woods, I've heard
the sweet ascending triple word
echoing over
the silent river —
but never
    seen the bird.

The Greater Forest

At root, at deep root they meet,
the honey-locust out at McCoy Creek,
the Valley oak above the barn
at Kishamish, the large-armed
horsechestnut that stood on our street
towering with white torches in late May,
Coast Range firs that green the wind with pollen,
dwarfed and gnarled flowering plums
of childhood, all of them, fallen
or standing, ancient forests before Rome
and shadowy woodlands yet to come,
they rise from the same deep root,
leaf out in the one light of day.

Red Alders in March

A bronze gong struck once
hums so long your ear
can follow the tone on
into out of hearing.

When the trees stand close
first hung with catkins,
that's how the color
of alders is: a ghost of light,
a rust-rose pallor, tone
so soft you catch it,
lose it, follow it almost
into out of sight.

Pinus Sabiniana

Digger digger ugly digger
trash tree   crooked tree   weed tree

Three long needles
greenish silver-grey
spring from a little scaly reddish cup
Three elegantly bending long and gracile
pine-leaf-needles a thousand
thousand times repeated springing
out of the scaly grey-brown twigs and branches

A heavy dense and large and sticky cone
carries the sweet tiny pine-nuts
deep inside itself and fast
in a small tight yellow shell that will not
break unless hit just right very hard

The digger pine lives only
about what a horse lives, twenty, thirty years
Grows fast like a poet or a weed
not very tall, maybe forty, fifty feet
Thrives on the soil called serpentine
where many soft plants wither
Grows up with its angular irregular branches
and harsh-scaled trunk and thousand thousand delicate
fountainlets of triple needles long and curved
and silvery in sunlight, in twilight

Foggy pine
Misty pine
A hillside of you will catch the sudden sun
in a sudden vast glittering
or one of you lift up its cloudy needles
against the fall of night
the moonlight dawning silver in it

Moony pine
Weedy pine
brief pine   grief pine   tear-filled
beautiful   dear   disregarded tree

Creation of the Horse

The salt green uncle-god, the Earthquaker,
thought of a creature with muscles like sea-swells
to leap across the beaches like a breaker
and beat on the earth like the waves with its feet.

So he struck a startled island with his trident
and then himself stood back in surprise
at the fiery uprearing, the white mane flying,
the foam-spattered flanks and the earth-dark eyes.

The Clydesdale Mare

She stands, her big white-feathered feet
planted in mud she's made by standing
always in the same place at the fence.
She stands embodying
the herd, her sister mares,
the big soft-eyed ungainly children
who sucked her milk and kept close by her side.
She is their absence now, those huge, heroic,
gentle horses, here in the empty pasture.

I think of them

all, their beautiful eyes,
gold and green-gold and beryl,
soft paces, silent presences,
the tail drawn across the wrist,
caress and blessing, the resolute
pursuit of comfort. All the floor
invisibly innumerably patterned
with four-petaled flowers. Laurel
crouched in the dignity of his agony
purring when I petted him.
Young Lorenzo poised cocky on a perilous
branch. A carton boiling over
with kittens, forty years ago. All the air
alive with ghostly leaps. We share the bed
with still, companionable warmths
through nights of how many winters
gone, dark now, and yet to darken.

Grace

The kitten no bigger than a teacup growls
true threat at interference with his food,
will bite the hand that feeds him, and draw blood.
They are entire tiger in their souls.
They shame the monkeyness in us, that howls
and grins and chatters and knowing bad from good
claims to be other than the animals
and nearer than the tiger to the grace of God.

Raksha

I think I could turn and live with animals, they are so
  placid and self-contain'd . . .
Not one is respectable or unhappy over the whole earth . . .

— *Walt Whitman,* Song of Myself

It's raining pretty hard in San Jose
and it has been raining
and will rain till late April, early May.
It isn't cold here. Only wet.
Rain pelting on the roofless porch.
Under the bushes by the porch is mud,
the parking lot is pools on asphalt,
the lawn is grassroots in water.
She can't get underneath the porch
so she gets underneath the chair.
An old green-plastic-covered armchair
too wide for the front door
sits mildewing inwardly
in the porch corner,
and the cat hides under it
from the rain. From loud noises.
From people in the parking lot.
From dogs and cars and me.

She lived in this apartment before I did.
When her people left,
the woman upstairs says,
they couldn't find her so they left her.
She's a left cat. Sinister.

Piercing eyes. Demonic. Scruffy, longhaired,
black. All black. Hisses, spits, and runs away.
Bites, they tell me. Hasn't bitten me,
I don't wait to get bitten. But she flinches,
flattens, if I touch her fur
however lightly, furtively,
a foolish bid for bonding,
when I put down the bowl she runs to
fearful, distrustful, but hungry, hungry.
Wet, cold, alone, and hungry.
That's a cat's life, Walt.

I guess she chose to stay here.
Hid from her people. *Kitty-kitty-kitty,*
the car all packed—*Come on kitty,*
swing from the branches with us happy simians!
No, the cat said. No.
I know my place.

I call her Raksha, demon,
but she has no name.

I leave the door wide.
She does not come in.
Self-contained, but never placid,
she crouches near her refuge chair,
even in her sleep alert, aware.
I can't judge if she is or is not unhappy.
She's certainly unlucky,

less so than many cats.
She accepts, she does not beg.
She is wholly respectable.

While I'm here to feed her twice a day
she has some ease. When I'm gone,
if the next tenant doesn't,
well, she'll get bone-thin again,
get lame again, get sick and hide and die.
Or a car or a dog will kill her.

Turn as we may in our wonderful ease-making words,
we cannot co-opt her freedom.
We can live with her
only on her hard terms.

At the Clackamas County Fair

Eyes of rabbits, guinea-pig eyes are clear, black,
shining, watching. Ceaselessly watching. Splendid,
feathered bronze and silver, the grand prize rooster
    crows out his deathsong.

All the pigs are too much alike, the poor things,
pink tubes, bacon, barbecue. Sheep are patient,
firm. Two goats, their delicate heads together,
    comfort each other.

White the heifer, fair the girl of twelve or
thirteen, lying curled in the straw, the heifer's
drowsy trusting head in her lap; the girl is
    quietly weeping.

Extinction

Imagine dark.
Forty years' rain.
The sinking ark.

No dogs bark
or doves complain
in the long dark.

No eel or shark
noses in vain
the ribs of the ark.

No star, no spark.
No full or wane.
Silence and dark.

Without mark,
without stain,
bright, stark,

the ocean's arc
is bare again
above the dark,
the sunken ark.

III. Meteorology and Geography

Mendenhall Glacier

I never thought of a cold dragon
till I saw one dragging   its slow body
down the wide wadi   it had gouged
out of a mountain,   saw the bluish spatter
of icy water   from its mouth.
I'd felt the chill breath   long before
I came close and saw   it crawling there
half scaly, half bare,   dirty grey, old.
That breath was cold,   the hard breath
of a hard death,   a slow, cold death.

A Measure of Desolation

Again and again   the landwind blows,
sending back the rain
to the house of the rain.

Seeking, seeking   the heron goes
longlegged from creek
to thirsty creek.

They cry and cry,   the windblown crows
across the sky,
the bare clear sky.

From land to land   the dry wind blows
the thin dry sand
from the house of sand.

Coast Range Highway, November

Sky gloom and gleam.
Road rain-glaze glare.
Infinite light glitters
in fern-fronds, fir-needles,
flashes from great gold maples.

The local crow
patrols the road.
The local crow
knows.
And discloses,
reports, remarks,
speaks freely.
Though no doubt keeping
certain dark
secrets.

As the old oaks
are swift and shy
in their delicate flower,
so the reticent nobility
of the bronze oak autumn
lasts only briefly.
But the short-lived, long-leaved,
roadside willows will not
be hurried into gold,

and hold their green intention
to leaf out long before April.

The next rain crouches
in the yoke of the hills,
dark-grey puma
with a misty tail
lashing the silent
trees of the forest.

Seasonal Quatrains

EARLY NOVEMBER

Fog at the break of day and rain at the noon,
Days are getting darker to the winter.
Sun in the overcast weaker than the moon,
Days are getting darker to the winter coming soon.

DECEMBER 20

That great hinge of light up there
is just about to catch the red leap
of the year and pivot it right round
into the long evenings and open doors of summer.

FEBRUARY

The morning light slipped down the snowy mountain
quick and soft, a fall of petals of pink roses.
Already now the blue-grey shadow water
from lowlands and the misty foothills slowly rises.

SPRING NIGHT RAIN

A soft, immense commotion
wholly occupies the dark,
a murmur, a consolation
to earth, root, heart.

Morning in Joseph, Oregon

Its shadow briefly tracks a starling's flight
across the dotted line that shows the way
a cat went straight across the snowy lawn
last night when just past full the sinking moon
cast shadows eastward in the silent town
and turned the snow peaks ashen grey.

Sun shines, bird flies, snow melts, the cat is gone.

Hour of the Changes

A wild early April strangeness,
crazier than any autumn evening,
mild air full of flooding wind,
motions of storming branches,
a queer, creaky, crying sound
way off, as the rain advances—

What's that? a thud of thunder?
a big tree going down?
the sound of the untime after?
No, only the hour of the changes,
uncanny, oceanic,
smelling of hyacinth, ozone, daphne.

Summer Morning on the Volcano

The mist lifts off the little lake down there,
way down, across a gulf of shining air.

The upward spiral song of Swainson's thrush,
a white-crown's teedle-eedle in the hush:

there is this music in the morning, where
was only silence, and grey dust, and ash.

"We are her children, we are in her care,
our destroyer-mother," sings the mountain thrush.

For My Traveling Companion

Dun and blue levels come before my eyes
as if we still were driving towards the sun
that has not set, our journey is not done,
and we're still traveling under desert skies

out where the mind can find its proper size,
enlarge, stretch wide, be still, or freely run
like the cloud-shadows on the blue and dun
plains and far mountains under desert skies.

Up the Columbia

Where at the edges and backwaters of the river
lie inlets and shallows surrounded by rushes,
and over his perfect reflection the heron
beats the quiet air with long slow wings,
where redwings claim their dominion over the cattails,
and a frog crouches humble, immobile,
watching with golden eyes: there to that low world
of sand and mud and slow imperceptible currents,
of small changes and no change and endless renewal,
my mind returning recovers the sweetness, the refuge of morning.

Navna: *The River-running, by Intrumo of Sinshan*

(The form, called in Kesh wukada yepewóya,
*"laboriously repeated coming-and-going," is uncommon.
The meter is* klev wedai, *"first of four.")*

Listen to the voices of the water in its going.
Quiet as an outbreath as it wells up in its spring
deep in dirt among the stones, it gathers up its flowing
and creeps out into daylight like a little living thing.

Almost it is silent, as it wells out from its spring.
Azalea-shrub and willow have their roots in its beginning.
Coming into daylight out of shadow, the quick thing
murmurs a soft dancing-song, the music of its running.

Azalea and scrub-willow have their roots in its beginning,
but down among the digger-pines and oaks it takes its way,
singing in a stronger voice the music of its running,
deeper ever downward through the hills toward the sea.

Now among the vineyards and the fields it goes its way,
from all the springs and all the creeks it gathers in its flowing
deepening and slowing through the marshlands to the sea.
Listen to the voices of the River in its going.

At Kishamish

September 28–October 7, 2010

THE CORNER ROOM

I am back in the old house on the hill,
daughter, grandmother, sister, ghost. The feet
I follow are my children's feet, and mine.
Who is the child in this empty room that grieves?

So little moves the air the live-oak leaves
quiver only now and then. The grey-green pine
semi-stunned hangs in the silence of the heat.
I had forgotten how this place is still.

LATE SEPTEMBER BIRD

There is a big discussion going on
down in the oaks around the barn.
The council of the acorn woodpeckers
proceeds with yells and laughter, squawking, purring.

Up here by the house, less is occurring.
The hawk flies over with a peevish curse.
The towhees hold quite still. Then they return
to ground-work. The one wren is here and gone.

There is a bird I wish I knew; at dawn
it sings three notes, just while the day is born,
a falling cadence, sad, and yet it stirs
delight in me intense almost past bearing.

THE KNOCKING

The birds have fallen silent. A loud, deep,
intermittent, hollow knocking sound
comes from the barn. Not the woodpeckers' fast
snare-drumming. This is something bigger.

A messenger, a prisoner, a beggar,
the wind gusting, an owl, a restless ghost.
Or all of those. This is a troubled ground
where old and unborn spirits wake from sleep.

TURKEY VULTURES

The bird books always say they have no voice.
Maybe they say nothing in most places,
but who else could be making that rough,
faint croaking in the woods up there?

Maybe they're dumb where we make so much noise
and only speak in such rare quiet places
as this, where I hear now the slow huff . . . huff . . .
of wide black wings that loft through silent air.

THE MOUSE-COLORED DOE

The doe walks with almost a pause
after each step, lifting each delicate
leg up like a marionette;
she hesitates without apparent cause,

flicks her big ears again, goes on
through the high barren grass of early fall
serene, unhurried, and aware of all
that threatens her or she can live upon.

JUAN DOLORES

My mother told, when I was little, how
I'd grab his finger, my hand being too small
to get a hold on his, and shout, "Go? Go?"
And Juan would go at baby pace beside me

up to the road gate—fifty yards in all—
a mighty expedition for me then. And now,
eighty years later, again I find it so.
O for the patient, big, dark hand to guide me!

TURKEY VULTURES II

Maybe they don't say anything because
they know more about death than anyone,
so intimately that they needn't talk about it
among themselves. And no one else wants to hear them:
they're smelly, shameful, ugly, don't go near them.
And so they keep their quiet company, uncrowded,
and sweep great silent circles in the sun
to praise the lord of life, his ways and laws.

THE EVERYDAY

First light. The arc of the old moon was rising
in a windy dawn that quickly grew behind it.
Silver-bright at first, it dimmed and thinned
till it was lost in a vast radiance.

What happens every day is what's surprising.
The treasure's never where I look to find it
but where I simply look — the sky, the wind,
sunrise, a silver arc, the moment's chance.

AUTUMNAL

Sun's hot, breeze cool, autumnal. Dragonflies
appear on wide transparent wings, and soar,
and disappear. Down among oak-world shadows,
dark tapestries of leaf and arching branch,
the little redhead clown birds flit and start.

It's strange to see these hills with present eyes
I hold so clear in my mind always, strange once more
to hear the hawk cry down along the meadows
and smell the tarweed, to be here — here at the ranch,
so old, where I was young — it hurts my heart.

ACORN WOODPECKER

Bright black-and-white, a bright red head, a bright
mad eye, he looks in from the windowsill
three feet away, but doesn't see me. Now he tries
the frame for grubs, finds none, flits to the oak,

gets himself perched and firmly braced upright
by bending in his tail, begins to drill,
works hard a while, and then flick, off he flies.
Bird of my heart! half holy and half joke!

THE CORNER ROOM, II

An hour or more yet till the sky turns blue
and the first sunlight strikes across the hills.
It's cold, it's still, and lying here I'm free
to drift among the years, float on their flowing.

A child could climb out the north window to
the crotch of the big oak whose foliage fills
the east window. It was a sapling tree
when this was Betsy's room. Oaks are slow growing.

IV. Developmental Ontology

At the Center

If the intrepid hero with his flashlight
should get through the trashy
outskirts to the door to the corridors that
wind and clamber in my mind, and force
his bright lightbeam through crumbled
intentions and forgotten passions encumbering
attics and blind basements, and get finally
to the oldest, inmost chamber, he will find
no minotaur, nothing frightening,
nothing even to shine his light on,
only the deep smell of dry grass
and dry adobe of an August hillside
when you lie down on it face down
breathing into and out of that one place
in the long, kind, warm dusk
after sunset and before the stars.

Early Memory: Jocken

First things lie deep, here in the starting place,
unseparate, composted into ground.
I come here without much hope to find
anything but the once bright images
gone dull with overuse: the jeweled dress;
the yellowish gravel of the garden path;
a redwood wall; quiet water in the bath
reflecting walls and window upside down,
so I was frightened, but the fear is gone.
Only a sense of how intense things were,
how near and piercing, and how dear
the round, still eye, the short, dun, silken fur.

The Merchant of Words

The little now is all I ever knew,
this seaport city of my years,
this shore I walk on, that the tides
gnaw as the sea rises and keeps rising.

What can I tell of what occurred
before my birth, that foreign, sunrise land?
I cannot know it, though my isle
was once a part of it. I used to watch
the long, bright caravans creep down the roads
from fabled mountains, out to the promontory
of the morning where my city stood.

Those roads are long since undersea.
We only have what drifts to us from there
over dark waters: fragments
of carven wood, a hollow green glass globe.
Some papers in a sealed chest
in a strange writing, half effaced.
A storm-blown bird, whose song
receives no answer here.

I sent my ships to rumored western lands,
heavy with hopeful cargo.
And for a long time they returned
laden with wine and honeycomb,

silk, linen, opals, amethysts.
The sailors sang as they rowed in to harbor.
All they brought they laid out on the beach.
I went in splendor in the city then.

Few ships go out now, few come back, and those
are empty, dancing on the waves.
What can I tell you of that other country
from which my caravels return
so lightly, with thin sails that let light through,
and thin sides, and grey-haired sailors,
and the broken amphorae empty?

Stammersong

Let
let me
let me be
Set
set me
set me free

Own
only
only soul
Lone
lonely
lonely whole

Sigh
silence
silencing
I
island
and I'll sing

GPS

I've flown as far as tern or heron fly,
clear to the polar waters, and returned.
I've run the roads of land and sea and sky
right round the earth's horizons. So I learned

that there are two directions, out and back,
from the still center of the compass rose.
There are two places: home, away. I lack
a map that shows me anywhere but those.

The House Is Soft

The house is soft, softly carpentered.
Even the nails are yielding, semi-transparent.
People come in one by one
and live there a while, quietly feasting,
and leave by the door they entered.
They leave the house forever but not empty.
The passages of the house remember
and the windows look not only out
but inward to the tender rooms.

Seven Lines to Elisabeth

Come back my daughter and make me another
mild posole, two anchos but no jalapeños.
Play Bach on the cello. Make me a mother
again as you did many years ago now.
Reawaken the old house with music and tears.
Whatever you do, always you do it wholly.
O child come back, make me another posole.

Final Destination

Ogives of ice-lines on the airplane window
soften to water in descending sunlight.
How shall I know what I have done right,
what I should do, what I should undo,
lost daughter, wanderer, coming home so late?

Ghazal at the Oasis of Mara

The doves cry of lust and sorrow in the oasis.
I will be gone tomorrow from the oasis.

Great palms comb the water with their fronds,
a gesture of grace to borrow from the oasis.

The desert is dry and wide and easy to die in.
The paths are short and narrow at the oasis.

How green my heart still is in my old age!
Are the paths all dust I follow from the oasis?

Long ago a young man killed a mourning-dove
with a slender palmwood arrow in the oasis.

Sometimes they called Oorsoo, Oorsoola,
the dove-voices, soft and hollow, in the oasis.

Travel

A little child's travel is from life to life,
vague green transitions, April into May.
A teddybear for luggage, no idea of direction.

Later comes apprehension, the fear that I
must die to all I was in going far away,
and the heavy bags to open for inspection.

But they seem lighter at every border crossed.
You learn to be without the need to stay.
Only at the last stop is the dear toy lost.

Then there's no travel. No traveler.
No way, no one to go or fear. There never were.

Pillowtalk

Are you asleep? We lie here hearing
the rain in the dark. I want to ask you,
Why is it all so strange?

I'm sleeping and dreaming of the rain
in the dark, in the dark ground.
I'm ranging out, ranging far.

You're lying here beside me
as you've always lain.
But it all keeps changing, changing.

Is it your voice or the rain
I hear like somebody weeping?
Lie easy, love. We're out of danger.

Low Barometer

Some days something wants and wants to cry
but it can't get out and be aloud,
pressed down by the silent heavy cloud
    all day not going by.

Some days everything goes wrong,
the diagnosis and the conversation.
If patience is the only virtue of the patient
    how shall we suffer song?

My Birthday Present

Seventy-nine, seventy-nine,
I say it over, and every time
it sounds peculiar. Is it a prime?
It's a queer number, seventy-nine.
I will enter my eightieth year
tomorrow evening somewhere near
six o'clock, around dinnertime,
my mother told me. That's a queer
hour to be born, or to enter an eightieth year.
But all of it's queer, being here.
Thinking how what I thought was mine
was only borrowed, and what was dear
has been forgotten, and every line
I've written will become a sign
for nothing at all, given time.
But that's what I was given, time.
That's my present, present time.

The Arts of Old Age

written in the airport

I learn the arts of old age day by day:
the expertise of being lame; the sense
of unimpatient impotence;
the irony of all accomplishments;
the silent, furtive welcome of delay.

Sometimes it seems

Sometimes it seems so deep, the emptiness
    within an open grave.
Yet earth fills it with earth. No loss makes less.
The rising wave lifts from the hollow wave.

The earth is deep, and sweet; my heart's at fault
    for seeing any waste.
But still the sea is salt, and tears are salt.
Sometimes it seems that salt is all I taste.

The Body of the World

on the train between Seattle and Portland, October 2009

I am this body and the leaves I see
blown from the brassy cottonwoods
beside the road. The body of the world,
the mountain and the clouds above it, that is me.
I breathe the autumn wind that is my breath
and in my body lives my brother, dead
two days ago. The one thing I am not
and he is not nor can we be is death.

When They Came

Four armored men on gaunt white horses rode
up to her open door and straight into the hall.
She saw her rooms shrink narrow that were broad,
the spacious windows darken and grow small.
The pocked man flicked his whip across her back.
She cowered down and then could not stand up.
The tall one drew his sword, stooped to the door,
and slashed away the doorknob, bolt, and lock.
The thin young fellow stuffed into his sack
her silver bowl, her flowered china cup.
Horse-hoofs beside her gouged and scarred the floor.
The fourth man's iron finger stopped the clock.

Hindsight

How different people are when they are dead.
How changed is what they did, what they said.

What we think we know and what we know—
Eliza leaping terrified from floe to floe.

So cold, so fast the river, yet last spring
it went soft, slow, in lazy wandering.

"Why do you turn your back on me?" I'd cry,
not noticing how few you looked at eye to eye.

Across the swift dark current voices call.
The warm words slow, and freeze to snow, and fall.

You fought so bravely to escape from slavery,
and all along, the whole time, you were free.

Body of Water

Waking at dawn I am a river flowing,
an earthen bed with a body of water in it,
my being all a constant onward going.
A silent scarlet flick of digits glowing
nearby reports the change of hour and minute
and the velocity at which I'm flowing,
but time as number has no way of showing
directions that a motion might be headed.
Where it comes from tells better where it's going.
Sometimes I wake up easy and I'm floating,
being the water and a little rowboat on it
carried along on the easy steady flowing,
other days I rouse up hard, supposing
danger, a rapids, and the rowboat in it
thrown about and blind to where it's going.
But with no oars there's not much use in knowing
about the rapids; I'll drown in it, or run it,
I the boat and bed and rocks and river flowing
and ocean end of all and onward going.

Aubade

Few now and faint the stars that shone
all night so bright above you.
The sun must rise, and I be gone.
I leave you, though I love you.

We have lived well, my love, and so
let not this parting grieve you.
Sure as the sunrise you must know
I love you, though I leave you.

Votum

Let it be clear, a clear day
from the eastern ridges to the sea.
Let the oak be dropping
its long fragile flowers
onto the ground under the branches.
Let no cloud gather in the sky,
no wind disturb the fall of the flowers.
Let the shadow lie under the branches
silent on the ground.
Let the oak outlive me
by a hundred flowerings.

V. Philosophy and Theology

Finding My Elegy

I can't find you where I've been looking for you,
my elegy. There's all too many graveyards handy
    these days, too many names to read through tears
on long black walls, too many bulldozed bonefilled ditches.
    And all the animals to mourn, wiped off
the earth like mist wiped off a mirror, leaving one
    face, reflection of itself alone,
image of its imagined image; nothing else,
    no grief, no dirt, no dogs, no elegies.

That desert is no place for you. And so I looked
    where death is birth and gods are animals
and being flows through being as from the spring the stream
    flows to and through the rivers to the sea;
but what's to mourn, if life betakes itself into
    another life? Better a rite of passage,
painful joyful celebration of the change,
    warning and welcome to the soul returned
forgetful who it was, and we not knowing either,
    seabird or child, salmon or fern or fawn.

And on the eightfold way, although compassion finds
    itself at home, all the hard work of sorrow
dissolves to breathing in and out the lives let loose

from turning turning turning, gone nowhere
to do no harm at last, after the long despair.

    So where to seek? I used to dream of climbing
high in the hills, those silent ridges red with dawn,
    to find your sisters the Laments; but that's
a hero's journey. I am older than a hero
    ever gets. My search must be a watch,
patiently sitting, looking out the open door.

    Far off through shadow I can see a woman
who stands to speak a name. Though I can't hear her voice
    across the ruins of the centuries,
I know how hard it was to speak, how her throat ached.
    In Rome, beside the pyre or open grave,
they'd say the name aloud three times, and then be still.

    A name is hard to say. Who'd read aloud
all those names on that long wall? What woman born
    could bear to know so many children dead?
Numbers are easier. So the men of money say
    numbers, not names. Grief's not their business.
But I think it may be mine, and if I have
    a people any more, I will find them in tears.

    My elegy, your clothes are out of fashion.
I see you walking past me on a country road
    in a worn cloak. Your steps are slow, along

a way that grows obscure as it leads back and back.

In dusk some stars shine small and clear as tears
on a dark face that is not human. I will follow you.

The Whirlwind

Will fear of the foreboding dream
avert or invite the prophecy?
How to foretell the paths of dust
caught in this visionary whirl,
this standing wind, this spiral stream?
A breath breathed out will set me free.
I'll choose to do the thing I must.
The world dreamed me, I dream the world.

Intimations

Why is it I want to cry?
Crow, crow, tell me.

There is a shadow passing by.
The willows call me.

Why would an old woman weep?
Willow, tell me, willow.

Crows went flying through my sleep.
I cry and follow.

Some Mornings

Some mornings I'm a door on the top of a hill
swinging a little to and fro, without a frame.

When I was a high room made of wood
sunlight slanted down the air to the empty floor.

It's good to be what I have been before
and to be only air is also good.

Some mornings there's no reason for a wall
or a roof, or a hinge, or a word.

When gravity draws me right down to the core
things rest in there without a name.

Breathing the dark air in I almost understood
that soon I would breathe darkness without air.

This morning for just a moment being
was the moment and becoming all.

In the Borderlands

The part of this being that is rock,
the part of this body that is star,
lately I feel them yearning to go back
and be what they are.

As we get closer to the border
they whisper sometimes to my soul:
So long we've been away from order,
O when will we be whole?

Soon enough, my soul replies,
you'll shine in star and sleep in stone,
when I who troubled you a while with eyes
and grief and wakefulness am gone.

Jewel and Gravel

I. BLUE MOONSTONE

Years wore a bloom on this soft stone,
    fogging the vivid blue
    until it can shine through
only when I hold it up against the sun.

Time works a veil across the eye
    that dims the world's color,
    turning brightness duller,
until imperishable diamonds die.

So age ungreens the emerald,
    and fades the fiery ember,
    till mind cannot remember
what crimson was, and azure is annulled.

Yet what we know is what we own.
    Till dark takes everything
    I'll still wear my dull ring,
knowing the sky is hidden in the stone.

2. DIAMOND GRAVEL

I said that what we know is what we own.
So tell me whether I am rich or poor.
Is this a diamond or a common stone,
this fact I've learned, this truth I've always known?

Truths like the flesh decay; rock facts endure;
the little we can know is all we own.

Isn't our science hypothesis alone—
to seek for proof, yet leave it never sure
that diamond is indeed uncommon stone,
since there might be, beneath another sun,
miles of diamond gravel? Where's the cure,
if only what we know is what we own,
for poverty of mind?

            Add one to one,
make two; what wealth do you need more?
Coal and diamond are one common stone.
The chancy flesh stands up on certain bone.

What if my wealth's uncertainty—the power
to know that all I own is the unknown—
the diamond hidden in the common stone?

Science

What little we have ever understood
is like an offering we make beside the sea.
It is pure worship when pursued
as its own end, to find out. Mystery,
the undiminishable silent flood,
stretches on out from where we pray
round the clear altar flame. The god
accepts the sacrifice and turns away.

Tout rêve . . .

(Victor Hugo)

Everything dreams; but what may be the dreams
of matter we can only make a guess,
whose minds are all a mist and maze of names
where matter is unsubstanced in the word.

Maybe the hearthstone dreams the mothering fire
that shaped its darkness, or it drinks the cool
of ancient springs; maybe it hears the choir
of stars, and dances where it lies unstirred.

A fallen forest fills the long house-beams
with shadows and the sound of wind-borne leaves.
The cedar-branches laid upon the pyre
sing, remembering a singing bird.

The sleeping sea moves, restless with desire.
Its black abysses pulse with half-shaped gleams.

Morning Star

. . . wenn ein Glückliches f ä l l t . . . —Rilke

Only in downfall is grace offered?
Upward-outwelling fountain
and water-spring sink to follow
down the ways and passes,
folds of furrow, channel, suffered to go lower,
lower yet, to descend the sacred.

O graveness! O most open!

Not outcast but willing, the light
of the star bright as falling water
blessèd in falling blesses.

Uncaged

A square wood room with a square screened window
that looks out on the oaks, the barn, the hills of summer:

there I first said, why worship anything but this? —
and was uncaged to sudden, utter freedom.

Sixty years later, I stand at that square window
and see the barn, the oaks, the radiant summer,

and the hills my heart goes up to
as the bird goes, joyous, guideless.

A God I Know

A god I know moves very slowly.
Not like Zeus's lightning crack
or Satan's cell phones.
No. He travels like an inchworm
measuring the eternal terms,
and every inch is holy.
He goes slowly and often he turns back.
I know him only in my bones.

January Night Prayer

Bellchimes jangle, freakish wind
whistles icy out of desert lands
over the mountains. Janus, Lord
of winter and beginnings, riven
and shaken, with two faces,
watcher at the gates of winds and cities,
god of the wakeful:
keep me from coldhanded envy
and petty anger. Open
my soul to the vast
dark places. Say to me, say again,
nothing is taken, only given.

The Conference

Some time between the beginning and the end,
who was it called, what great lamenting voice?
A word rang out across the inner sky
of jeweled zodiac zone and sailor's star,
across the close-shored seas, the long-known lands,
to come, to meet in council in eternal Rome.
And while the pope sleeps warm in downy satin,
and homeless folk as always huddle cold
on Roman cobbles, those who were summoned here
from counted centuries and chasms of time
gather together.
               They are not manifest to mortals,
though sleeping pigeons tuck their heads in tighter,
and children dream strange dreams. Pilots aloft
look down through dark to not quite see
the dome of Peter glimmering with glory,
flicker of myriad wings of candleflame;
a tired night-watchman by the Tiber almost hears
the ruined temples under ground groan welcome.

They come: those who are called the Living, those
forgotten and called dead: but in their presence
is life still, and all things are remembered.
The two that walk apart are here, apart,
Allah, Jehovah, each one with his book;
and Jupiter whose mantle is the sky
and all its weathers, comes with his thunderstone;

and Zeus the stern seducer; the one-eyed Wanderer,
two ravens on his shoulders, with his staff;
Jesus healed from wounding, his ghost-winged dove
and blue-robed mother following modestly;
Freya with her beasts; the Many-Breasted One;
and striding, implacable Athene; and then, clear
and sudden as in summer with the wind
of dawn the young light strikes across the sea,
Aphrodite comes, and the stones of Rome
tremble with fierce desire at her coming.
The Lady of the Crossways, dark and bright, is here,
and goddesses of trees and hidden springs,
and shaggy sinuous river-gods, Pan leaping like a goat.
Down from the northlands pace the druid powers,
shadowy lords of the great fallen forests.

The gods of Egypt stalk with head of cat
or hawk or vulture, in white pleated linen,
narrow of waist, with long and narrow feet.
The bright lord of the Farsis blinds with flame
the dull-eyed, cruel idols. And slowly, one
by one, innumerable images
of clay and stone and bronze crowd silently
from storehouse, gateway, kitchen, army camp.
Old, crude, fat, headless Venuses of chalk
out of the barrows and the shallow graves
come in their ancient dignity of awe. So all the streets

and ways and open places of the city
are filled and shiver with fullness of immortal being.

So it is everywhere: for in the City
of Mexico blood starts from the pyramids:
the Plumed Serpent and the Turquoise One have met.
The lion of great stones that is Cuzco rises, scenting
from the altars of Machu Picchu smoke of copal,
and Pachamama strokes the dark head of the lion.
Who dances on the ashen steps the Ganges washes,
where a million forms of the long dreams of Vishnu
gather in conference? Who comes to the drum-call
through jungles, over Africa's long plains,
and who to Coyote's quavering cry across the desert?
Corn Woman rises, and with White Shell Woman
walks in beauty, and the tall kachinas
stride through the streets in silence to the kiva.
The gods are gathering in all the hallows,
Ayers Rock, Kuala Lumpur, and Stonehenge,
all deities in all their names and aspects,
a flood that follows darkness round the world,
luminous, intangible, and countless;
and as it is in Rome it is in all sacred places.

The first to come, who is also the last,
opener and closer of the door, speaks from
his two mouths: "What is to be done?" he says.

The voice
is like a great wind blowing in the darkness,
like a warm breath. The gods are that breath.

God is that wind. It answers: "Mourn."
The anger of God gathers in the night,
a stormcloud deploying: "Have I not destroyed them
    in their iniquity, before?"
The power of God bursts forth in a scream
of steel, a burst of blinding fire: "War!"
The mercy of God murmurs, "Forgive them."

But it is Aphrodite born of ocean foam,
Corn Woman risen from the furrowed dirt,
Persephone daughter of the bread men eat,
with her dark-crowned husband, and the shadows
of all the lives that lie in earth, who answer
without a word. It is the mortal Earth
herself, who breathes the being of the gods,
whose long warm sigh blows all the words away
into the silence that was always there.

    The city falls. It takes a day
to fall, or centuries. The seven hills
stand for a while longer.
                    Prayers are spoken,
sung, breathed out; was there once an answer?
The conference is over. Dust blows across the mesas,

lies on the altar, fills the bowl of stone.

    The poles grow blue and dark.
Low shores surrender to the sea. Islands go under.
Over drowned Mumbai and Bengal
the sun sets with a red grin like Kali's.
Insatiable Tlaloc has had his fill at last.
The web Anansi wove hangs loose, a cobweb.
The roofs of the world collapse, Himalayas, Andes
flow down in torrents of barren rock and water
as thick as Shiva's hair, as bright as Inti was.
White horses charge from the despoiled ocean,
salt manes blowing, hoofs trampling, destroying.
No hand is on their reins to guide them.

There were places and their names and gods.
There were those who inhabited this house.
Across the sands of Libya a hawk flew hunting,
past the red mesas a lean coyote trotted,
a hummingbird in Nicaragua flared like a thrown ruby.
Over the broken Yangtse dam did dragons soar,
did raven or phoenix nest in rubble of cement
and rusted steel beneath the Golden Gate?
These names are named no longer. Voices
are few and far between, they are strange voices,
the mouths that speak have changed their shape,

and who is there to tell us the meaning
if a word is spoken?
          If it is not in the end,
it was not in the beginning.

          The poles whiten, spray of iron oceans
grows stiff as styrofoam; islands arise again with steep
cliff-coasts of stone; ice groans in the great silence.

Among the many ways and other worlds,
galaxies of galaxies, immense vibrations,
quiver of atoms, quanta, passage of kalpas,
the Earth goes on her changing circling way,
dancing her dance of turning and returning,
sweeping her shadow down the shores of light,
maker of darkness, mother of the night,
whose children too cast shadows where they go.

Index of First Lines